I haven't been myself lately and I hope the
future is as good as I want it to be.

OTHER BOOKS BY ROBERT M. DRAKE

Spaceship (2012)

The Great Artist (2012)

Science (2013)

Beautiful Chaos (2014)

Beautiful Chaos 2 (2014)

Black Butterfly (2015)

A Brilliant Madness (2015)

Beautiful and Damned (2016)

Broken Flowers (2016)

Gravity: A Novel (2017)

Star Theory (2017)

Chaos Theory (2017)

Light Theory (2017)

Moon Theory (2017)

Dead Pop Art (2017)

Chasing The Gloom: A Novel (2017)

Moon Matrix (2018)

Seeds of Wrath (2018)

Dawn of Mayhem (2018)

The King is Dead (2018)

For Excerpts and Updates please follow:

Instagram.com/rmdrk
Facebook.com/rmdrk
Twitter.com/rmdrk

ISBN: 978-1-7326900-1-1

Book Cover: Robert M. Drake
Cover Image licensed by Shutter Stock Inc.

For The Lonely.

CONTENTS

MOON MATRIX

ROBERT M. DRAKE

CAUSED YOU

You understand
my darkness.

You understand
what hurts.

Maybe you've got
the whole goddamn universe
inside of you…

and maybe every shooting star
is a tear
made of all the pain
I might have

caused you.

TO BE TO BE

They say
to be brave,
to have no fear,

that fear is the devil's
greatest illusion,

but this I tell you
about fear.

Never trust those
who fear nothing,

those who say
they're not afraid
of anything.

Fear is life,
for fear is what pushes

the average person
toward greatness.

The fear of not
making ends meet.

The fear of losing
your mind.

The fear of losing
your job.
The fear of failure.

The fear of death.

The fear of
the unknown.

And the fear of losing
the people you love

among other things.

Fear can make both
men and women
do miraculous things.

Those who fear
not making ends meet
find possibility
in darkness.

Those who fear
losing their minds
find genius
in the rubble.

Those who fear
losing their jobs

find bigger paths
to bigger opportunities.

Those who fear
constant death
find life
for what it truly is.

Those who fear
the unknown
find themselves
in the most beautiful
of places.

And those who fear
losing the people they love
always find them
when they feel most alone.

Fear is beautiful.

It keeps people on the edge
but too much of it
can be deadly,

too much of it
can shut out the light.

You need just enough
to get you going.

Find the balance.
It is there
within you.

Have fear
when it is needed
and have no fear
in between.

One love.

BLOOMING

Believe
that some
beautiful things

do grow
out of the darkness.

So please,
swallow the moon

and let it bloom
from within.

The shine awaits.
The gods await.

And the chaos
of the heart will be
balanced.

Believe
that some
beautiful things
grow

out of the darkness.

Believe

that light
always

comes
from within.

EVERY TIME

Love me.
Care for me.
Cherish me.

Despite who I am
or what I have done
or who I am meant
to be.

Remember me
for all the seashells
I left on your shore.

Remember me
for all the footprints
I left on your sand.

Because I was here once
and parts of me
will always be with you,

just think of me
every time you feel
the need to shatter.
The need to start again.

I will be waiting…

in the same place
you saw me last.

YOU HAVE TO

You have to love
 before you hurt.

Break
before you heal.

This is how it works.

This is how
you become whole
again.

CANDY THOUGHTS

Sweet misery.

The man said
they couldn't get along.

That she was crazy
and always had something
back to say.

He said how much
he loved her
but also
how much
he would destroy her,

that is…

if he could.

They couldn't get along
from the start.

Well,
I will say this:

you can't destroy
what you've never understood,
so to put things

into perspective,

she's a wild river
and you're just another person
who's in love
with her violent waves

but is
far too afraid
to swim.

Women, like men…
cannot be tamed.

They should not be
controlled.

Freedom is always
the answer,
my sweet people.

COMPANY

Let my words
keep company
to those who feel
lost.

With those
who feel
like they don't know
who they are.

My words will never
keep their distance.

They will always remain.

The light
the human heart
radiates
is not defeating.

It starves the darkness
and feeds the sun.

The connection
between us all

is everything.

WOMEN FROM THE PAST

Women all over,
flooding the Earth
in search of their souls.

I see these women,
bright and beautiful,

some even
with the goddamn sun
flaring out
of their chests.

They have swallowed
the sky,
the stars and all things

that make the very moon
believe
that the darkness
is a lie.

These women,
smart enough to champion
the hearts
of the broken.

Strong enough
to make buildings cringe

and collapse.

Brave enough, these women
to split their own lives
to birth life.

These women,
these sharp,
contagious women.

Some even have
more stories
in them
than the books
technology has buried.

And some
have what it takes
to change lives

while others are torn
with creating
their own path.

These women.
These women.

These spider-like
women.

They all have me,

trapped on the web,
every single one of them.
They have my soul.

My breath,
blood, sweat, pain
and they hold it
as if
it is their own.

I put trust in them.
I trust them with the riots
in my skull,
even with the ones
in my heart.

The waves of love crash
as I am rocked to sleep.

These women,
I adore them.

I write about them,
for them,

my thoughts are born
from the spawn
of their flowers.

Overthinking,
overanalyzing,

over society
and over the way

I see the world
but never am I over
these women.

They remain king
of all kings.

I see what everyone
cannot see.

I see these women,
but the problem with these women
is that
they do not know
how to touch the human heart
without grabbing
the human body.

They think they are free
but the walls they build,
defeat them,

collapse over them
and put most of them
in hard positions
they do not understand,
let alone know how to
get out of.

Things hurt, especially,
when things fall.

And we all fall but

these women.

These women.
These women.

They are not like her.
Like the one who saves me
every night.

The one I rest with
until the afternoon.

The one who knows me
more
than I know myself.

Without her,
I cannot find the clear.

I cannot see
through the hands
that cover my eyes
from the truth,

from the despair

that molds me
into gold.

I see her.

This woman.
This woman.

This

little

joyful

woman.

In all glory,
drunk and in love,

freeing me
from all the pain
my country
and its people
have caused me.

She makes me
love myself.

She makes me
want to do better.
She makes me

feel familiar things,
things I once felt
during my youth.

She's a child,
my child,

a piece of all the things
that make me.

A collection of my pain,
my love,
my heart,
my tears
and my laughter.

She takes me away,
far from this place
with all her God-given talent
and restores

whatever is left
of me.

I hold her now
to believe,

that maybe one day,
when I am old

she will hold me

the same way
I held her in my arms.

She gives me peace.
She gives me life.
She gives me all the things
I never knew I had.

I love her now,
in the past

and in the future.

Seven times,
to the moon
and back.

OCEAN SHORE 2

You were always happy
near the water

and I swear

I'd trade my wings
just to let you swim

in the ocean again.

ALMOST TRUE

The sad truth about people.

No one wants to hear
about what worries
other people.

No one wants
to do enough
about their pain.

What worries other people
is not their concern,

at least

not until
it affects them.

So when you see death
and violence all over the screen...

deep down
your heart will say

*"Damn, someone has to
do something about it."*

And then

your mind comes
for a second opinion
and adds…

*"Yes, someone,
but that someone
will not be me."*

Everyone wants change
but no one wants
to do their part

to create the change

we all want
for ourselves.

NEVER WANT

And still,
after everything
I've been through,

I still don't understand myself.

For every time
someone left,
I caught myself chasing

after them…

and every time
someone stayed,

I caught myself
ignoring them
a little more.

And there was never
a balance
between the two.

The more they took,
the more I gave

and the more they gave,
the less I took.

People are strange.

They never want
what is given to them

and

they always want
what they don't

deserve.

INSIDE IS WHAT COUNTS

I fall in love
with the paint
not the painting.

With the people
not the places.

With the religion
not the church

and with the flowers
not the garden.

The same way
I fall in love
with her soul,
not her body.

With her touch
and not her skin.

With her smile
and not her lips.

The things
that make her
who she is

make me
fall in love

even more.

BEWARE OF YOUR ART

Beware of those
you spill yourself to,

for someone,
many moons ago
granted me

a revelation.

They said
that the fakest people

are the ones who brag
about being real.

It is true
and I add:

You should never brag
about what you have.

You should never do
things with half a heart.

You should never take
opportunities
and people for granted.

You should never put
down others.

You should never think
you're better than others.

You should never give in
to the system.

And you should never
say never
about your dreams.

Be you.
Do you.

You fuck with yourself
more than anybody else.

And always remember,

people know
what crap smells like.

They could tell
the difference

between lilacs
and dog shit.

So please

don't be one of those
people.

Understand
that legacies are built
off action

and not

a steaming pile
of empty words.

SHE INSPIRED ME

She had
a certain way
about her.

The way she spoke,
the way she moved
and thought.

She inspired people
and made them feel
as if
they were loved

and understood
again.

DO NOT MISS THE POINT

That's the point.

You have to let things
slip away.

You have to stand still
and watch them go

far enough
to see if they return.

You have to know
that all hellos
turn into farewells,

that the space within you
always breaks apart

no matter how long
you've held it together.

And once you've experienced
this,

the way good things vanish
at any given time.

You understand…

and soon after,
you understand

how there are some things
you can't recover from.

How sometimes
loving someone

is the greatest gift
to ever receive,

but also

the worst curse
to ever feel.

Even when you know
it's not meant to last
at all.

Everything is worth
your time.

Everything.

Everything.

Everything.

Do not ignore things.

Do not let them die
throughout
the night.

GO TO BED

Sometimes

I cannot help
but to wonder

what you're thinking of

when you first wake up
and whom it is

you are missing
by the time

you go to bed.

HUMAN LIFE

Human life is difficult
but also very precious…

and out of a billion
star systems,
we exist.

So why,
tell me why
do we destroy one another.

Tell me why
we must go to war
with our neighbors
and those
we don't find a connection with.

Tell me why
things happen the way they do
and tell me why
none of us seem
to get along.

So why,
tell me why.
Why can't we live in peace?
Why can't we find it
in us

to understand ourselves?

To understand each other.

To make sense
of our differences,
and to
respect one another
and carry on.

Remember this:

What you do now
will affect the future
in all shapes and forms.

Remember this:

This is our moment,
your moment
so please be kind.

Remember this:

Everyone matters
and every person you don't know
is going through
the same hell

you are.

And lastly, please
remember this:

Humans are born to love...

so smile at strangers.
You never know whose life
you're meant to save
or change.

Human life is complicated
but it doesn't
have to be difficult.

NO GOOD-BYES

The worst good-byes
are the ones
without closure.

You never forget
the last time
you saw them

and that's
what haunts you
the most.

LET HER…

You could start
and end wars…

devour the moon
and watch the Earth
slowly burn.

You could pull the clouds
out of the sky…

let go of gravity
and watch the mountains
crumble.

You could drain the oceans dry,
destroy what people stand for
and spit on their beliefs,

but please,

for Christ's sake,
let her go.

Do not hold her
within herself.

She can be so much more
that is,

if only she believes to be.

If she believes in herself.

Let her run.
Let her swim,

and let her fly
toward the tip of her
young imagination.

Let her be,
let her shine
and let her

forever

fan the flame
from the dying
of the light.

Let her breathe
among the stars

and let her find
what she came for
before her time

is done.

Let her.

Let her.
Let her.

Let her conquer
her own heart
and let her lose
whatever doubt she holds…

to rise anew…

like a rioting
wild flower.

Let her begin,
and begin,
and begin,

all over again.

LETTING THEM GO

The real tragedy is
loving someone
while knowing

they're no good to you.

And letting them go,
believing
you were never

enough.

MY DEAR

My dear,
I know when we are
together
we believe that

by some miracle
we can save
each other,

that our wrongs
can make a right,
and if we remain

through the painful nights,
we will grow.

My dear,
I know when we are apart
we believe
that the flowers
in our hearts
stay madly in love,

missing the sway
of our stars.

My dear,
I know

that before we met,
we couldn't love
one another
as we were,

that we had loved
one another
before
we became who we are.

My dear,
I know that if there is
no you,

I am a hostile man
in search of me,

that without you
there is no me,

that I don't know
who I am
without you.

My dear,
I know
that the more time
I spend with you
the more

I wildly expand

beyond the thin margin
of life,

that you are
the death of me
and that I'm okay
with dying

as long as I die
happily by your side.

My dear,
I know
when I think of my past
it only means
I am closer to my future,

to the other life
where you and I

find one another
to relive the chaos
between man
and woman.

My dear,
before I finish
this letter,

I want you to know
that all the above

I feel deeply,

that all the above
I believe
with my bones.

That all the above
is the lava
in my veins

and you,
my dear,

are the center
of it all.

TO MY DAUGHTER

And when
I am no longer here…

when my bones
have filled the ground
and my inspiration
has touched the youth…

remember,
always remember,

when a butterfly lands
on your shoulder,

that is me,
reminding you,

of how much
I truly *miss you.*

SEE YOU, MAN

I want to see you.

I want to tell you
how I, too,
carry the same pain
and suffering.

And believe me,
I have enough of it
in me,
perhaps, enough
to kill me,
to kill us,

that is,
if we gave it
the chance to.

But you,
now there is you,
and I would like to
see you again,

to tell you
how you made my life
worth living...
from the core
of my body

to the marrow
of my aching bones.

I love you
and I am grateful
for who you are.

Come back soon.

IF IT DOESN'T

If it doesn't feel right,
then lose it,

even if that means
losing people.

It should always be
mind over matter.

Humanity over politics.
Peace over war.
Love over hate.

And please,
make mistakes,
learn from them,
and never forget

to follow
what the heart

desires.

SEARCHING FOR MORE

It's when you begin
to look for answers
and meanings
when you lose all sense
of direction,

of where you're meant
to go.

And it's the same way
with love and people.

The moment
you begin searching,
is the moment
you've lost all hope.

And it always happens
when you feel
as if
you're getting closer.

For example,
you take one step toward love
and love takes five steps
away from you.

And it also works

like this:

When you don't have,
you want
and when you have,
you ignore,

that is,
until it drifts away.

So if you want
a fair shot,
you've got to ignore
the things you want
and things
you think… you need.

You've got to
open your heart
and feel,

let things happen
on their own, you know?

What's meant for you
will come for you

and what's not
will walk right by you,

like the thousands of people

you see
but are never meant
to meet

at all.

THE PAST IS A SHADOW

Some people
spend their lives

trying to solve
why others leave.

And I cannot help
but wonder
why some people

cannot accept
the past

and move on.

SAY SOMETHING

You should say
what you feel.

Not because
it is the right thing
to do…

but because
the next time we meet

I might be
a different person,

and you might not
recognize me by then.

Therefore,
you should always say
what's in your heart

because it might be
your only chance
to do so.

The words
that belong to your life
are only written once.

Do not let them
go silent.

The moment you do,
you're doomed.

A BOY

A boy comes up to me
and says I am his idol
and that I am a genius.

I am flattered
but I am far from both.

I do not know how to write,
let alone spell.

I do not know
what I am thinking

most of the time,
let alone feeling.

I do not wish to be
anyone's idol.

I don't know how to be.

I don't know anything, really.

I'm just someone
who's been through enough,

who's had enough.

I'm just someone who never
took *no* for an answer.

From people
and goals to dreams.

I have always chased
what was mine.

I have always worked
a little harder

to do all the things
I've wanted.

I've lost sleep,
friends, and family

at the cost
of my aspirations.

And I expect people
to do the same.

That is,
if they really
want it.

Never let go of a dream.

Make it happen,

die trying.

Reach it,
even if it kills you.

Even if that means exile.
Even if that means

perfect isolation.

Always chase
what is meant

for you...

ALWAYS.

Always.

Always.

No matter who says what

and no matter

who gets in your way.

SO WILL YOU

When someone has been
in your life,
they become a part of you.

And when that person
is gone—they take
a part of you with them.

And from then on,
you will never be
the same person as before.

The things you once ignored
will stand out more.

The stars will shine brighter.
The oceans will roar
a little louder.

The air in your lungs
will fill you more.

Everything around you
will change,

and so will you.

COLTON AND JEFF 2

This is the beginning
of your new life.

The first day
of a long awaited dream.

Take it in.
Inhale.

Everything you've been through:

Every moment—
perfectly synchronized
to prepare you
for what's next.

For the long life
that awaits.

A life filled with laughter,
happiness
and endless joy.

This is the beginning
of something beautiful.

The beginning
of memorable moments…

where the sun
and moon collide.

Where two lives,
two flames,
two hearts,

crash and greet
upon the shore.

This is the beginning,
of where your hands
will no longer have to wander.

Where your heart
will be someone else's home
and it will never be left empty.

It will never be left abandoned.

This is the beginning,
the breath of fresh air,

the moment you let go
to land into the ocean.

That split second between
life and death.

Between love and friendship.
between your past

and your future.

What once was
and what will soon become.

This is the beginning
of your new life.

The spark.
The stars aligning.

The feeling
of what it's like
to love one person
forever.

This is your time,
Your moment.
Your life.
Your future.
Your honor.

Your goals
and your dreams.

And you are blessed

because…

you have not just chosen
to spend the rest of your life

with a lover

but also,

your bestfriend.

Congrats,
my brothers.

IN THE WORLD

I want you
to meet good people,

fall in love with them,
you know?

Because I care
and I know,

sometimes,
I look too much
into things

but it's because

I know you deserve better.

And I know
you know too.

I know the sun
and the moon aren't enough
for you,

and I know
you hide your scars
with constellations.

I know so many things about you,
therefore,
I know what kind of life
you deserve,

what kind of people,
you know?

I want you to find
the reasons to love yourself
again—to heal again

and make sure happiness
to finds you.

Because you matter
and self-love

is the most

inspiring thing
in the world.

THE PAST MEANS NOTHING

You haven't changed much.

Although
you believe most of you
has gone away.

You're still the same person
you were.

You're still shy,
kind, and soft as ever.

You're still young
and beautiful.

Reckless
and full of life.

So I am not sure
why you feel this empty,

why you romanticize loneliness
and make love to all the broken parts
of yourself.

Those things aren't you.

Those flaws don't define you

or make your future
any brighter.

I know your past hurts,
but there's no reason to live there.

There's no reason
to plant flowers

in a place that hasn't been fertile
for years.

Your history doesn't dictate
your path.

It shouldn't direct you
toward darkness,
toward complete isolation.

I think you choose that
for yourself

but like I said,
it doesn't have to be
this way.

There's still
so much light in you.

So much sun,
moon and space

to be filled.

So much love
to hold
as your own.

My god,
you are so beautiful,

and the way you love yourself
is the most precious thing
in the world.

I just hope you realize this

before
it's too late.

STAY WILD

Appreciate yourself.

Don't let people
make you believe
that you're a mistake,

that everything you feel
is wrong.

Because most people
don't even know
what's good for them,

and most of them
are looking for themselves
in all the wrong places.

So I'm not sure
why some of them feel

as if

they have the right
to dictate your life.

The right to tell you
how to feel.
Because everyone has

a different role,
a different agenda,
you know?

So how you see things,
how you love,
cry and feel

will never be aligned
with someone else's way
of being.

This is your life.

Your love,
friends and dreams

and they only belong
to you.

So appreciate them
for what they are.

Water them.

Give them a little sunlight
from time to time

and watch everything you need grow.

And don't be afraid

of disappointment
because in the end,

it all means something,
and it all happens to push you forward,

not to keep you buried
behind walls.

So stay free,
my friends,

stay wild
and stay

crazy…

dizzy in love.

THE SECRET

Here's a secret.

Those people
you compare yourself to
are secretly comparing themselves
to you.

So I wouldn't worry
about other people

because

no one knows anything.

Everyone is trying
to make sense of themselves

by seeing
what others do.

FALL APART

Regardless
of how you feel—
of how broken
your heart is,

no one really wants
to be left alone.

Everyone needs
someone to talk to.

Someone to pour themselves into.

Because it's completely healthy
to shatter from time to time.

It's completely normal
to feel nothing sometimes—
to be okay
one minute and completely
destroyed the next.

That kind of thing
is going to happen,

it *MUST* happen.

But still,

there's no reason
to isolate yourself
because you feel different.

The strongest people
WILL crumble

but their friends
and loved ones

will collect
their pieces,
will put them back together,

and hold them—whenever

they feel
the need to fall apart.

ART YOU UNDERSTAND

Most people
will never understand you.

They will never
feel what you feel

when you listen to a song
or when you pick up

an old photograph.

Most people don't feel
as deeply as you.

They don't feel
what others feel

nor understand
why people like you
exist.

And because of that,
most people

will *exile you.*

Feed you to the wolves.

They don't want to hear it.

They don't want to
understand or even try.

People are lazy.
They don't have

enough time to learn
new things,

to understand
new people.

But you...
you're different.

You care,
although everyone tells

you that you shouldn't.

But that's
what makes you, you.

You have this intensity
flowing out of your eyes

and you don't give a damn
what others say.

You feel
what you feel

because you must.
Because the human heart

is the only art
you understand.

NO GENIUS HERE

And now,
I am supposed to be

some kind of genius
but only because

I have written down
what I've felt.

I've used my words
to express my thoughts
and heart.

And it is not
that I am some kind
of super hero.

Far from it.

It is just
that I speak the truth,

directly from me
to you.

I've seen bad days
turn to good days

and good days
turn to bad days.

I've lost
to find

and I've found
to lose again.

It is a cycle.

It all comes back again.

I inhale to exhale.
I sleep to wake.

I fall to rise.
I love to feel unloved.

This is how it happens.
It always has.

I've just learned
to write it down.

This is the cost of living.

To experience
and pass it down.

And to be honest,

I've just learned
to tell the difference

and the similarities,

between my life
and theirs,

and it doesn't take

a goddamn genius
to realize that.

EVERYONE IS NO ONE

Everyone
is always telling you
what you deserve.

You deserve
someone to love.

You deserve
a good life.

You deserve
a good job,

a good night, etc.

How about
you deserve
to be yourself,

to be

who you want
to be.

To love
who you want
to love.

Even if it kills you
slowly from within.

You deserve
what you desire

most

and nothing more.

ROUGH WORLD

It's a rough world
and some people save you

from it
the moment you meet them.

They'll make you feel
as if you can fly

without ever leaving
the ground.

As if the stars
are on the palm

of your hand…
and not the night sky.

Some people make you feel
as if you have

an infinite number
of second chances

even if you don't believe it
for yourself.

I MET A WOMAN

I met a woman
one day

and she told me
she loved me.

Her sweet smile.

Young
like the dreams I once had

and tamed
like the love I've been sold.

I met a woman
one day

and she told me
she loved me.

Her skin soft
like the cotton balls

my mother once used
to bless her soft skin

and her eyes
hazel brown

like the butter crunch
I held
on my hands as a boy.

I met a woman
one day

and she told me
she loved me.

With words that flowed
out of her mouth

like music notes
expelled from a saxophone

and with an attitude
so strong

it would make
a grown man cry.

I met a woman
one day

and she told me
she loved me.

With a heart
that's been broken
more than a dozen times—

fallen off several
burning buildings

and barely surviving
each time.

She has a way
with my very own

heart.

Hers is broken
and mine is anew—raw,

untouched
 and clean

like hot glass
fresh out of the kiln.

I met a woman
one day

and she told me
she loved me.

We spent hours together,
more than enough.

Wasted days,
months, years.

Lost like two wild animals
running afar from a forest fire.

I met a woman
one day

and she told me
she loved me.

I revealed my pain
like a man with nothing
to lose

and she held my secrets,
dreams and hopes

on the tip of her hands
like a child fiddling around

with a Christmas ornament.

They fall.
They shatter.

Explode like shotgun shell fragments.

My hands reveal
that I am made of flesh
and blood.

That I cannot carry

what weighs.

I met a woman
one day

and she told me
she loved me.

It hurts.

It all does,
like having my bones
pulled and my skin

stretched far
beyond my reach.

It hurts,
it always does.

Still does.

My body aches
from searching.

My soul burns
from aching.

And my heart breaks
from regretting.

I met a woman
one day

and she told me
she loved me.

All of my worries,
troubles, regrets.

All of my suffering,
healing and learning.

Everything I am.
All I have become.

Stronger.
Smarter.
Better.

It is owed to experience.

It is owed to all the women
who told me they once loved me,

but failed to keep their word.

I met a woman
one day

and she told me
she loved me,

and I told her,
I loved her in return.

And words
were all we gave
each other.

Too bad that was that

and

from there on out

we were *NEVER*
the same.

PRETTY THINGS

People want pretty things.

They want something
to help them forget

the harsh reality
they live in.

Something like theater,
music and poetry

to help them escape
their stressful lives.

And how beautiful it is,
that sometimes,

those aspects can be found
in another human being.

How sometimes,
you find someone,

and for reasons unknown
all you can see is art.

All you can feel
is the pounding of your chest

as they make you feel alive.

And that's the beauty of people.

Some of them
make you forget
while others heal you

and make you feel

something

when you need it most.

YOU ARE NOT READY

Sometimes,
you just aren't ready.

No matter how much thought
you've put into it—

how much enthusiasm
you have toward it.

Sometimes,
the right person comes along

and it doesn't work—

no matter how hard
you try.

No matter how much
you want it to.

So be prepared to lose
every once in a while.

Be prepared
to let go

and understand,

how sometimes
timing

is everything.

DO YOU

Do what makes you happy.

Is it too much to do.
Is it too much to live for.

Do what makes you happy.

There is no reason
to live for other people.

There is no reason
to impress people

who do not care
about your movement.

Your genius.
Your art.

Do what makes you happy.

People are going to
talk anyway.

People are either
going to accept
you or hate you.

They are either going to
understand or refuse to.

Do what makes you happy.

You deserve to be.

You owe it to yourself.

To the generations
who came before you.

The ones who gave their lives
to give you the life

you are living.

Do what makes you happy.

I cannot stress this enough.

Do not be
one of those people

the kind that does things
to be liked.

To be adored and praised…
to go home feeling empty
and alone.

Do what makes you happy.

You owe it to yourself.

To save yourself.

To find your smile
and share it
with the people you love
the most.

Do what makes you happy.

Do it. Do it. Do it.

Take a midnight walk.
Stay up late on a work day.

Binge on liquor, food.
Binge on life, love.

Do what makes you happy,
fucking do it.

I beg of you.

Take the risk.
Take the chance.

I urge you to care less,
to do things for you.

Don't think twice about it.

Do what makes you happy.

Die doing it,
chasing it.

But do it because you want to.

There is no other way
to kiss the sky.

WHAT IT OFFERS

If something is bothering you,
then it is bothering you.

You have the right
to feel terrible
when bad things happen,

and the right
to feel happiness

when good things happen.

Balance is key,
patience goes a long way

and timing

is *EVERYTHING*
this life
has to offer.

PARK NIGHT AND DAY

Because self-love
doesn't sell papers.

Self-improvement
doesn't break media records.

These things
are ignored.

My god,
where did it go wrong?

We glorify self-mutilation
to feel beautiful.

Praise the celebrity
to promote self-hatred,
self-doubt.

The beauty companies
want us to believe
that we can never be beautiful,

therefore,

we must buy
what they sell.
The pharmaceutical companies

want us to believe
that sickness is everywhere,

therefore,

we must inject our children
with their vaccines—

to weaken
the human body.

We are sick,
deranged and lost.

All hope
is almost gone.

But some of us are
still fighting the good fight.

And others know
about the war

but do not know
how to defend themselves.

These are the hidden secrets.

Do not buy into
what they sell.
Do not become

a slave.

You are beautiful.
You are perfect.
You are healthy.

And they rely
on *YOU* to survive.

On *you* to keep going.

The rich get richer
while the poor stay poor.

And these industries want you
to join their subscriptions.

They want it all:

your mind,
body and soul.

So please,
do not fall

into their trap.

Take this with you
and save yourself

while you still can.

END WITH YOU

I don't know my future.

Hell,
I don't even know
what I'll be doing next week,

let alone next year.

So I can't make
any promises…

but I do know one thing.

No matter where I am,
what I feel
or who I become.

It will always

begin and end
with you.

SO MUCH YOU DO NOT KNOW

You have so much
to look forward to.

So why do you keep
going back

to the same people
who don't appreciate you.

You know,
the ones who keep telling you
they'll change but don't.

It's almost like
you don't care

about yourself, kiddo.

As if
you don't love yourself
enough to move on.

So you keep putting yourself
into these hard situations

in the name of love—thinking
it'll end well,
only because of love.

Because of how much time
you've invested.

It doesn't have to be this way.

You don't have to
put up with it,

although
you *think* you do.

Real relationships don't work this way.

You don't give
to expect something in return

but you also
don't give

and expect nothing.

It's all for something.

It always is.

And it's hard
and confusing,

I know
but it works both ways.

You love
and expect to be loved
in return.

It's simple.

Anything else
is you,

not giving yourself
what you already know

you deserve.

Amen.

WE BLAME OURSELVES

We blamed ourselves
for what happened between us.

For the way
things ended,

for the way
it hurts.

We blamed our timing,
our age and where we were.

Shit…

that's a lot to take in
but it's true, my dear.

The odds were against us.

Not one star was aligned
when you gave,
and I took and vice versa.

Never on the same page.

Always to our necks—
crazy and in love.

But as all things,
all good,
beautiful things…

it didn't last
long enough.

We let each other slip away
and blamed who we were
at that time.

Two kids lost in the frame
of broken love.

I now sit here,
fifteen years later

and reminisce of our time.

Turn up my head phones
and listen to sounds in my head.

To the way
we used to make love.

To the way
we used to break up

to get back together again.

And now,

shifting through the years
we spent together…

I now understand
why things happened
the way they did.

You were too young,
and so was I

and our love
was *too much* to bear.

We held on,
believing it was forever,

and soon enough,
we ended

too soon.

Sometimes people
step out of your life

quicker

than the way
they came in.

And too often
do they vanish

into thin air
and all you're left with

is one question…
it goes:

"Why couldn't I do
a little more
to make you stay?"

NEVER TOO LATE TO...

It's never too late
to change your mind,

to find... to let go

and realize

what type of person
you deserve.

Because one day,
you're going to finally
meet someone

whose entire universe
will revolve
 around you.

Until then,
keep doing you

and know
with every fiber in your body
that you

are not hard to love.

TRYING TO HEAL

I'm still trying to heal
from all the things

I have yet to understand.

Trying to move on
from the people

I could have had
but slowly saw them

walk away.

THOSE MOMENTS

We've all had those moments
when we thought it was the end.

We've all been there before.

But I'll tell you this,
when was the last time

you felt this way?
And when was the last time

you moved on?

You'll get over it.
You'll find your peace.

You'll learn from the past
and hopefully

you won't let history repeat itself.

Experience is a *motherfucker*
but it is also

your greatest teacher.

Amen.

HEAR FROM YOU

I want to hear from you.

I want to wake up
to a text from you—

to a missed call.

I just want to know
what you've been doing

and I want to know
if you're okay.

REASONS UNKNOWN

And for reasons unknown,

it hits you the hardest
at night.

The overthinking.

The stress of things
you can't change.

It hurts,
and sometimes

it feels like you're drowning
but you'll survive.

You'll live to see
another day

and laugh

over all the times
you thought it was the end.

WHO MATTERS MOST

One day
you're going to realize
who matters.

One day
you're going to have to let go
and move on

 just to see
who comes back to you

but not because
you want them to

but because they need to.

One day
I tell you,

the one you deserve
will be the one who stays.

And there's nothing better
to look forward to

than that.

WHO HATES

People who hate you
are going to hate you

no matter what you do.

But the goal is
not to prove anything to them.

The goal is
to make them feel you.

Make them open their eyes
and realize

that hate
is the down fall of humanity.

That hate
is such a pointless little thing.

People who hate you
don't *really* hate you.

They've just misjudged you
because they haven't had

the chance
to understand.

GETTING HURT

Don't be afraid
of getting hurt.

Be more afraid
of never having someone

to come home to.

Of never having someone
worth missing

and of never telling someone
you love them.

So go for it,
be soft with it.

Getting your heart broken
should be the last thing

on your mind.

HAPPY RUNS

It is sad
how some people leave
the ones who try to make them happy

but run towards
and fight for

the ones
who always seem
to hurt them
the most.

MORE THAN YEARS

It has taken me years
to understand

how important solitude is.

Being alone is one thing
but being with someone

and feeling alone
is another.

And I rather be by myself
than be with someone

who makes me feel
even more alone.

WHAT GOOD IS LOVE

What good is a love
that isn't shared.

A love that isn't
received back.

Is it only really worth it
when it is exchanged?

When it is only felt
between the two parties.

What good is love
when it is not shared

and what good is it
to be alive,

if I live a life
without you.

THE RIGHT WORDS

You always have
the right words to comfort me.

The right way
of calming me down.

I love you for this.

You have no idea
how much I do.

Although,
words cannot express

what it is you make me feel.

I just want to keep telling you
how much

I apprecite you
and our friendship.

That's all.

SOMEONE YOU LOVE

What you make me feel
will never get old.

The heart has no time.

You make me laugh.
You make me smile.

And in a lot of ways
you have saved me.

I know this will never be enough
but I must try.

I love you
but not just any kind

of way.

I love you.

And the last song
will be sung.

And the last kiss
will be given.

And the last moment

will be shared.

And we will learn
how our love

is an art

and the masterpieces
we will leave behind

will change our children's
children.

I love you…

and I can't say it enough.

I love you
and let this be my last word

if my soul ever departs
from my body.

This human experience
is meaningless

if you do not share it
with someone

you love.

COMING BACK

I hope you don't plan
on coming back

because once you're out of my life...
you're gone.

And I hope
you don't expect me

to be around either.

You're not allowed to fly
towards the stars

if you've given up
your wings

for a chance to swim,
and you can't expect me

 to save you
from drowning

if you've given me every reason
to never

look back.

WHAT YOU CANNOT SEE

Sometimes
you never see it

coming
until it hurts you

and you never know
how much

it means to you
until it's gone.

BEING ALONE

My solitude has made me
realize many things.

1. Not everyone will love
with the same intensity as me.

2. People come and go,
and they are only a few
who are meant to stay.

And

3. My health and well-being
comes first,

everything else can wait
and everything else

can be solved
with a little patience

and a little time.

ADVICE ADVICE

Everyone
keeps giving you

advice

but no one
is willing to take it

for themselves.

The same way
everyone knows what's best

for them

but no one
is willing to fight

for what they deserve.

THE SAD PART

The sad part is,

you might spend
the rest of your life

thinking about them,
wondering what happened to them

and how different your life
could have been.

The good part is,
you have the choice to move on.

The choice
to forgive and forget,

and most importantly,
the choice

to learn from it
and leave it all

in the past.

YOUR TIMING IS EVERYTHING

Trust your timing.

Trust your gut feeling.
It is all for something.

Know it when you see it.
Go for it before it is gone.

Trust your energy.

If it is telling you to go
then go.

If it is telling you to stay
then stay.

No one *knows* better
than yourself.

And any advice should be appreciated
but the choice is *yours.*

Therefore,
if it feels like home

then you should always follow
its path.

And if it doesn't
then let it go

and know,
how something worth it

is

on the way.

BEST THEY CAN

You have to admit
when you're wrong sometimes.

You have to accept
your actions

and own up to them.

You can't do people wrong
and expect them to do you right.

You can't keep bringing up their flaws
and expect them to forget yours.

That's not how it works.

Be fair.
Be open-minded.

Be kind
and be respectful.

People are people
and every one of them

is doing
the best they can.

YOUR HEART

Don't ever let anyone tell you
what to feel

and don't ever let anyone
change your path

or influence your dreams
and goals...

because people
can change overnight

and decide to leave you.

So be careful with your thoughts.
Be careful with your heart.

Don't waste your time
for no one

and *do* what makes you happy.

That's all.

PRAYERS TONIGHT

You're in my prayers tonight.

I want God to guide you.

To give you light
when you need it most.

To give you the space
you need to breathe—

when you need to
expand your wings.

You're in my prayers tonight, baby.

I hope God touches your soul
and gives you hope

when you feel like
you've broken

your beautiful heart.

MEANINGS & WHAT YOU MEAN

The best is still
yet to come.

Just make sure
you don't cut off

the wrong people.

And make sure
you keep everyone

who has their best
interest in you.

And don't forget
to let things happen on their own

and don't force anything
either.

Because the moment you do,
is the moment

everything meaningful
is lost.

KEEPS US ALIVE

Sometimes you just can't win.

If you care too much,
you'll hurt yourself

and if you care too little,
then you'll hurt them.

This fact is hard to swallow...

wounds heal
but loneliness is forever

and yet,
this is the kind of place

we live in.

We give too much
and get too little

and if we get too much,
ironically,

that makes us care a little less
than before.

Love is *meant* to hurt

and I am almost certain

that the pain
is what keeps us alive.

NOT HERE

I don't want your love
if it's not loyal.

I don't need it
if you're not giving me

your all.

You can't expect me
to be real with you

if your heart isn't 100% there.

I don't need the moon
during the day

and I don't want the sun
at night.

I want balance.
I want what I put in.

If I love you,
then I expect the same

in return.

And if I give you my soul,

then I want nothing less
from you.

FEEL AT HOME

Some people want peace
and tranquility

and cannot find it.

Some people want
to be filled and unbroken.

And some people
just want to be held

and loved and feel it deeply
within their souls.

Everyone is searching
for something

and most of us
cannot explain it.

Most of us
don't know why we want

the things we want.

We just feel it
and spend our entire lives

looking...
searching...

for the things
that make us feel

at home.

CHEATED ON

We've all been cheated on
and lied to.

So there is no reason
to continue to let it happen.

We should always learn
from our past

and we should never let
the same things happen

more than once.

You shouldn't be hurting
over something you *could* predict.

You should be avoiding it
before it happens

and you should
be letting it go

before it begins
to weigh you down.

WHO WE ARE

Sometimes our choices
say more about who we are

than what we say
about ourselves.

SO MANY SAD PEOPLE

There are so many people
who feel alone.

So many people
who need someone to talk to.

So many of them
with so much in their hearts

and have no one
who'll listen to them

when they need it most.

Pay attention.
Give someone your time.

Give them your ear.

Give them your patience
and attention.

Listen to them
even if you have nothing to say.

That alone can sometimes
be enough to save a life.

And that alone
can sometimes be

what they need.

YOUR OWN BUSINESS

You have to mind
your own business sometimes.

You have to accept the fact
that you can't save everybody.

That you can't
solve everyone's problems.

You have to understand,
that sometimes

not getting involved
is the best thing you can do.

That sometimes
letting things settle

on their own
and not interfering

is the only option...

because sometimes
it can actually make things worse.

That's all.

BE KIND TO YOURSELF

Not letting things
get to you

will solve half of your problems
and letting things go

will teach you
how to accept your greatest losses.

It will make you appreciate life
and people and moments...

for what they truly are.

Be kind to yourself.

This is my message to you.